Space

Astronauts

Charlotte Guillain

www.raintreepublishers.co.uk
Visit our website to find out
more information about
Raintree books.

To order:

☎ Phone 0845 6044371

📄 Fax +44 (0) 1865 312263

💻 Email myorders@capstonepub.co.uk

Customers from outside the UK please telephone +44 1865 312262

Raintree is an imprint of Capstone Global Library Limited, a company
incorporated in England and Wales having its registered office at 7 Pilgrim
Street, London, EC4V 6LB – Registered company number: 6695582

Text © Capstone Global Library Limited 2009
First published in hardback in 2009
Paperback edition first published in 2010
The moral rights of the proprietor have been asserted.

Edited by Sian Smith, Rebecca Rissman, and Charlotte Guillain
Designed by Joanna Hinton-Malivoire
Picture research by Tracy Cummins and Heather Mauldin
Production by Duncan Gilbert
Originated by Heinemann Library
Printed in China

British Library Cataloguing in Publication Data
Guillain, Charlotte
   Astronauts. - (Space)
   1. Astronauts - Juvenile literature 2. Manned space flight
   - Juvenile literature
   I. Title
   629.4'5

Acknowledgements
We would like to thank the following for permission to reproduce
photographs: AP Photo pp.**16**, **22** (©Pat Sullivan); Getty Images pp.**6**,
11 (©NASA) **15**, **17** (©Space Frontiers/Stringer), **18** (©Stockbyte);
NASA pp.**9** (©GRIN/James McDivitt), **10**, **14** (©GRIN), **19** (©National
Aeronautic and Space Administration/Human Space Flight), **20**
(©GRIN/Charles M. Duke Jr.), **23a**, **23b** (©GRIN), **23c** (©National
Aeronautic and Space Administration/Human Space Flight); Photo
Researchers p.**21** (©Science Source); Photo Researchers Inc. pp.**4**
(©Pekka Parviainen), **5** (©Science Source/NASA), **13** (©Science Source);
Reuters p.**12** (©NASA); Reuters p.**12** (©NASA); ©UPI pp.**7**, **8**.

Front cover photograph reproduced with permission of NASA (©James
McDivitt). Back cover photograph reproduced with permission of NASA
(©GRIN/Charles M. Duke Jr.).

Every effort has been made to contact copyright holders of material
reproduced in this book. Any omissions will be rectified in subsequent
printings if notice is given to the publishers.

Contents

Space

Space is up above the sky.

People can travel into space.

Astronauts

People who travel into space are called astronauts.

Astronauts learn about space.

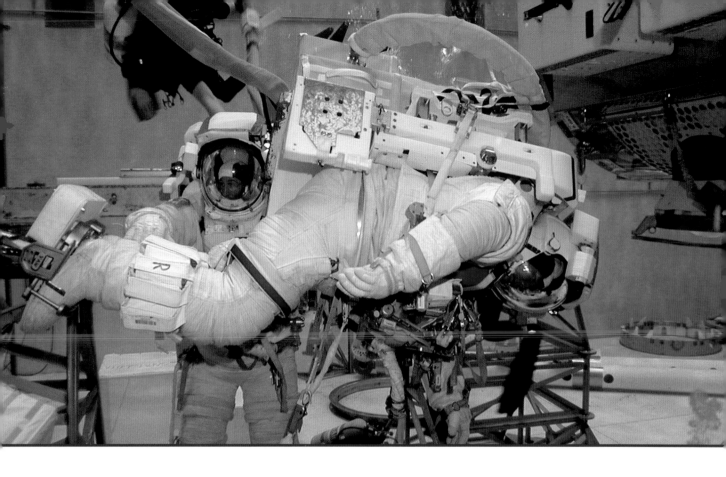

Astronauts learn to work in water.

This is like working in space.

space shuttle

Astronauts travel in a space shuttle.

The space shuttle takes astronauts
into space.

Astronauts can see Earth from space.

Astronauts float in space.

Astronauts wear a special suit
in space.

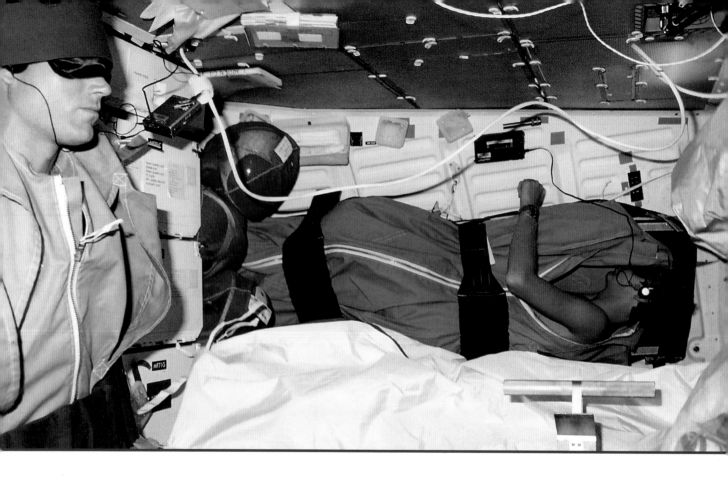

Astronauts sleep in a special bed
in space.

Astronauts have special food in space.

Food floats in space.

The space station

Astronauts are building a space station in space.

Astronauts live on the space station.

The Moon

Astronauts have visited the Moon.

They brought Moon rocks and dust back to Earth.

Can you remember?

What is this?

Answer on p.24

Picture glossary

 **astronaut** person who travels into space

 **space shuttle** vehicle people use to travel into space

 **space station** a place built in space where people can live

Index

Answer to question on p.22: Food that can be eaten in space.

Notes for parents and teachers
Before reading
Ask the children if they know what an astronaut is. Have they ever seen any programmes about astronauts on the television? What sort of clothes do astronauts wear? If they were an astronaut where would they like to visit?

After reading
• Make astronauts. Help children to draw round each other on large sheets of paper and cut out the shape. Use white or silver paint for the suit and coloured circles for the controls on the suit. Attach two plastic bottles to the back to represent the oxygen tanks. Suspend the astronauts from the ceiling or around the walls.

• Role play. Tell children that they are going to be astronauts and visit the planets. Tell them to put on their space suits and check they have their breathing apparatus. Take off in the space shuttle and visit Mars. Tell the children that it is very hot during the day but freezing cold at night. Look at all the red rocks and the enormous volcano. Continue visiting other planets before you finally decide to return to Earth.

World of Farming

Farm Machines

Nancy Dickmann

www.raintreepublishers.co.uk
Visit our website to find out more information about Raintree books.

To order:
☎ Phone 0845 6044371
🖨 Fax +44 (0) 1865 312263
✉ Email myorders@raintreepublishers.co.uk

Customers from outside the UK please telephone +44 1865 312262

Raintree is an imprint of Capstone Global Library Limited, a company incorporated in England and Wales having its registered office at 7 Pilgrim Street, London, EC4V 6LB – Registered company number: 6695582

Text © Capstone Global Library Limited 2011
First published in hardback in 2011
The moral rights of the proprietor have been asserted.

Edited by Siân Smith, Nancy Dickmann, and Rebecca Rissman
Designed by Joanna Hinton-Malivoire
Picture research by Mica Brancic
Production by Victoria Fitzgerald
Originated by Capstone Global Library Ltd
Colour reproduction by Dot Gradations Ltd, UK
Printed and bound in China by South China Printing Company Ltd

ISBN 978 0 431 19554 4
15 14 13 12 11 10
10 9 8 7 6 5 4 3 2 1

British Library Cataloguing in Publication Data
Dickmann, Nancy.
  Farm machines. -- (World of farming)
  1. Agricultural machinery--Pictorial works--Juvenile literature.
  I. Title II. Series
  631.3-dc22

Acknowledgements
We would like to thank the following for permission to reproduce photographs: Photolibrary pp.**4** (Cultura/Bill Sykes), **5** (Britain on View/Nature Picture Library), **6** (age fotostock/Javier Larrea), **7** (Design Pics Inc.), **8** (Pixtal Images), **9** (Mark Pedlar), **10** (imagebroker.net/Guenter Fischer), **11** (imagebroker.net/Markus Keller), **12** (Fresh Food Images/Maximilian Stock Ltd), **14** (Creatas), **15** (All Canada Photos/Russ Heinl), **17** (Pixtal Images), **18** (Oxford Scientific (OSF)/Martyn Chillmaid), **19** (Tips Italia/Tommaso Di Girolamo), **22** (Pixtal Images), **23 top** (imagebroker.net/Markus Keller), **23 middle top** (imagebroker.net/Guenter Fischer), **23 middle bottom** (Pixtal Images), **23 bottom** (Fresh Food Images/Maximilian Stock Ltd); Getty Images p.**21** (Warner Bros/Sergei Bachlakov); iStockphoto p.**20** (© Susan H. Smith); Shutterstock pp.**13** (fotohunter), **16** (Katharina Wittfeld).

Front cover photograph of a red tractor in a field reproduced with permission of iStockPhoto (© Branko Miokovic). Back cover photograph of a grape picking machine in Gironde, France reproduced with permission of Photolibrary (Oxford Scientific (OSF)/Martyn Chillmaid).

The publisher would like to thank Dee Reid, Diana Bentley, and Nancy Harris for their invaluable help with this book.

Every effort has been made to contact copyright holders of material reproduced in this book. Any omissions will be rectified in subsequent printings if notice is given to the publishers.

Contents

What is a farm?

A farm is a place where food
is grown.

Farmers use many different machines.

Tractors

A tractor is a farm machine.

tractor

Tractors can pull other machines.

Planting

plough

A plough is a farm machine.

A plough digs up the ground
for planting.

plough

oxen

A plough can be pulled by oxen.

manure

This farm machine spreads manure to help plants grow.

Growing plants

This machine plants seeds.

The seeds grow into plants.

water

This machine waters the plants.

insect spray

This machine kills harmful insects.

Picking plants

The plants are ready to pick.

wheat

This machine cuts wheat.

This machine picks grapes.

hay

This machine packs hay.

Caring for farm machines

Farm machines are very important.

Farmers must take good care of their machines.

Can you remember?

What does a plough do?

Answer on page 24